Big Machines At Work

Garbage Trucks

By Jean Eick

The Child's World® Inc. ◆ Eden Prairie, Minnesota

Published by The Child's World®, Inc.
7081 W. 192 Ave.
Eden Prairie, MN 55346

Design and Production:
The Creative Spark, San Juan Capistrano, CA.

Photos: © 1998 David M. Budd Photography;
      p. 15 © Niall Benvie/Corbis

Library of Congress Cataloging-in-Publication Data
Eick, Jean, 1947-
      Garbage trucks at work / by Jean Eick.
           p. cm.
      Summary: In simple text, explains how garbage trucks work and what they do.
      ISBN 1-56766-528-4 (library reinforced : alk. paper)
      1. Refuse collection vehicles--Juvenile literature. [1. Refuse and refuse disposal. 2. Trucks.]
      I. Title.
TD794.E33 1998
628.4'42--dc21
                                                                                              98-3130
                                                                                                CIP
                                                                                                 AC

Contents

On the Job

On the job, garbage trucks work hard in your neighborhood! They pick up your trash and take it away.

The big garbage truck moves slowly up and down the street. Sometimes the truck is on the job while you are still asleep.

Slowly, the truck goes to the next can.

Up and down the street the truck goes

until all the cans are empty.

Garbage trucks pick up bigger loads, too. The truck stops at a **dumpster**. Two long, mechanical arms on each side of the truck reach out. These arms are called **robotic arms**. The driver watches the arms on a video screen, called a **monitor**, inside the truck.

Jerk, jerk! Up goes the dumpster.

Quickly, the arms dump the trash

into the back of the truck.

Jerk, jerk! The arms pull the

dumpster down again.

When the box on the back of the garbage truck is full, the truck goes to a **landfill**.

There the box is emptied. Then the

truck is ready to pick up more garbage.

Climb Aboard!

Would you like to see where the driver sits?

Climb aboard! The seat is up high so the driver can see far down the street.

The driver uses a **joystick**, which is a lever that makes the robotic arms work.

The inside

1. The driver's seat

2. The joystick

3. The monitor

The outside

1. The box

2. The robotic arms

3. The dumpster

Glossary

dumpster (DUMP-stir)
A dumpster is a large container where people take their trash. Dumpsters are often used at schools, apartment buildings, or for businesses.

joystick (JOY-stick)
The joystick is a lever that controls the truck's arms. It is similar to the joysticks on video games.

landfill (LAND-fill)
A landfill is a garbage dump. Garbage trucks take your trash to the landfill, where big machines bury it.

monitor (MAHN-i-tur)
A monitor is a screen used to watch the action outside of the garbage truck. It is similar to the screen of a television or computer.

robotic arms (roe-BOT-ick ARMZ)
A garbage truck's robotic arms are long pieces of metal that move like arms. The driver has controls that make the arms move.